THE
DON'T
LAUGH®

CHALLENGE

2 Truths & a Lie

GiRLS
DON'T
FART
Edition

DON'T LAUGH CHALLENGE
• BONUS PLAY •

Join our Joke Club and get the Bonus Play PDF!

Simply send us an email to:

bacchuspublish@gmail.com

and you will get the following:

- 10 BONUS hilarious jokes!
- An entry in our Monthly Giveaway of a $25 Amazon Gift card!

We draw a new winner each month and will contact you via email!

Good luck!

Welcome to the ultimate lie detector game,

TWO TRUTHS AND A LIE: GIRLS DON'T FART EDITION!

How do you play?

- Grab a friend or sibling, and decide who will be 'Player 1' and 'Player 2'.

- Every round, Player 1 will start the round by reading the first set of statements to Player 2. Player 1 will then circle the answers Player 2 thinks are false. Use the guided instructions to pass the book to Player 2, and complete the rest of the round.

- Once you have both answered your questions, turn the page to check your answers and tally up your scores! The player with the least points will have to complete the End of Round DARE!

- In the event that both of you end the round with a tie, BOTH players will have to complete the dare!

- Play through all 10 Rounds and add up all your points to see who will be crowned The ULTIMATE LIE DETECTOR! In the event of a tie, continue to Round 11 - The Tie-Breaker Round where Winner Takes ALL!

- Most importantly, have fun and get ready to learn some fun facts
Let's get started! ⟶

ROUND

# PLAYER 1

CIRCLE THE FALSE STATEMENT IN EACH QUESTION.

Question #1

A. Butterflies can only see the colors red, yellow and green.

B. There are more than 5,700 species of crabs.

C. Unicorns usually live deep in the forest.

Question #2

A. Tiana and Mulan are the only right-handed princesses.

B. Women have a slightly better sense of smell than men.

C. Snails take the longest naps and can sleep up to 3 years without waking up.

PASS THE BOOK TO PLAYER 2 ⟶

PLAYER 2

CIRCLE THE FALSE STATEMENT IN EACH QUESTION.

Question #3

A. Some people dream only in black and white.

B. A newborn kangaroo is small enough to fit in a teaspoon!

C. Cinderella's shoe size was a 5 ½.

Question #4

A. Potatoes are 90% water.

B. Humans share approximately 50% DNA with bananas.

C. Lions feet don't actually touch the ground when they walk, they tiptoe all the time.

TIME TO CHECK YOUR ANSWERS! ⟶

ANSWER KEY
CHECK YOUR ANSWERS!

Question #1

B. There are more than <u>4,500</u> species of crabs.

 PLAYER 1 _____ /1

Question #2

A. Tiana and Mulan are the only <u>left-handed</u> princesses.

 PLAYER 1 _____ /1

Question #3

C. Cinderella's shoe size was a <u>4 ½.</u>

 PLAYER 2 _____ /1

Question #4

A. Potatoes are <u>80%</u> water.

 PLAYER 2 _____ /1

Round Total

TALLY UP YOUR POINTS! WHICHEVER PLAYER HAS THE LEAST AMOUNT OF POINTS HAS TO COMPLETE THE DARE BELOW.

 PLAYER 1 _____ /2

 PLAYER 2 _____ /2

DARE CHALLENGE

WITHOUT ANY MUSIC, DANCE AS CRAZY AS YOU CAN FOR 30 SECONDS.

ROUND

2

PLAYER 1

CIRCLE THE FALSE STATEMENT IN EACH QUESTION.

Question #1

A. Hummingbirds' wings can beat up to 200 times a second!

B. Apes laugh when they're tickled, much like humans.

C. Mustard was sold as medicine in the 1830's.

Question #2

A. It is illegal to own pet hamsters in Hawaii.

B. Rats teeth never stop growing.

C. The well-known stone, Opal, has been discovered on Mars.

PASS THE BOOK TO PLAYER 2 ⟶

PLAYER 2

CIRCLE THE FALSE STATEMENT IN EACH QUESTION.

Question #3

A. Jasmine is the youngest Disney princess, at the age of 14-years-old.

B. Vera Rubin, an astronomer, received the National Medal of Science in 1993.

C. Pocahontas is the only Disney princess with a tattoo.

Question #4

A. Male rabbits are also known as "bucks."

B. An ostrich can run faster than most horses.

C. Mice are sometimes called "sand puppies."

TIME TO CHECK YOUR ANSWERS! ⟶

ANSWER KEY
CHECK YOUR ANSWERS!

Question #1

C. <u>Ketchup</u> was sold as medicine in the 1830's.

 PLAYER 1 _____/1_____

Question #2

B. <u>Beavers</u> teeth never stop growing.

 PLAYER 1 _____/1_____

Question #3

A. <u>Snow White</u> is the youngest Disney princess, at the age of 14-years-old.

 PLAYER 2 _____/1_____

Question #4

C. <u>Naked mole rats</u> are sometimes called "sand puppies."

 PLAYER 2 _____/1_____

Round Total

TALLY UP YOUR POINTS! WHICHEVER PLAYER HAS THE
LEAST AMOUNT OF POINTS HAS TO COMPLETE
THE DARE BELOW.

 PLAYER 1 _____ /2

 PLAYER 2 _____ /2

DARE CHALLENGE

GO OUTSIDE AND DANCE
LIKE A CLOWN!

PLAYER 1

CIRCLE THE FALSE STATEMENT IN EACH QUESTION.

Question #1

A. Crocodiles are able to stick their tongue out.

B. Mary Agnes Chase is considered one of the world's outstanding agrostologists.

C. Puppies and kittens are functionally blind and deaf for the first weeks after being born.

Question #2

A. Hedy Lamarr was both an inventor and a well-known film actress.

B. People used to call insects the "Beasts of the Devil."

C. Men and women see colors exactly the same.

PASS THE BOOK TO PLAYER 2 ⟶

PLAYER 2

CIRCLE THE FALSE STATEMENT IN EACH QUESTION.

Question #3

A. The giant squid has the largest eyes of any animal in the world.

B. Pineapples take 3 years to grow.

C. Some lipsticks and nail polishes contain fish scales.

Question #4

A. Strawberry is the only fruit whose seed grows on the outside.

B. Your brain cannot actually feel pain, only the receptors around it can.

C. The highest wave ever surfed was as tall as a 15 story building!

TIME TO CHECK YOUR ANSWERS! ⟶

ANSWER KEY
CHECK YOUR ANSWERS!

Question #1

A. Crocodiles are <u>NOT</u> able to stick their tongue out.

 PLAYER 1 _____ /1

Question #2

C. Men and women see colors slightly differently, with women seeing more shades of color.

 PLAYER 1 _____ /1

Question #3

B. Pineapples take <u>2</u> years to grow.

 PLAYER 2 _____ /1

Question #4

C. The highest wave ever surfed was as tall as a <u>10 story</u> building!

 PLAYER 2 _____ /1

Round Total

TALLY UP YOUR POINTS! WHICHEVER PLAYER HAS THE LEAST AMOUNT OF POINTS HAS TO COMPLETE THE DARE BELOW.

 PLAYER 1 _____ /2

 PLAYER 2 _____ /2

DARE CHALLENGE

PRANK CALL YOUR BEST FRIEND.

ROUND

4

PLAYER 1

CIRCLE THE FALSE STATEMENT IN EACH QUESTION.

Question #1

A. Jane Goodall, the world's foremost expert on chimpanzees, was inspired by the book *Tarzan*.

B. A group of jellyfish is called a "flock."

C. The average person farts between 10-20 times a day!

Question #2

A. The dirtiest thing in your house is most likely your toilet seat.

B. Some perfumes use a rare kind of whale poop to achieve high-end scents.

C. The Nile crocodile can hold its breath for up to two hours while waiting for prey.

PASS THE BOOK TO PLAYER 2 ⟶

PLAYER 2

CIRCLE THE FALSE STATEMENT IN EACH QUESTION.

Question #3

A. The only food that is unable to rot is honey.

B. Cows have best friends and can actually become stressed if separated.

C. The cheetah is the most common wildcat in North America.

Question #4

A. Patricia Bath, the first African-American ophthalmologist, helped restore sight in people who had been blind for decades!

B. Elvis actually had red hair, but dyed it black.

C. In Tokyo, they sell toupees for dogs.

TIME TO CHECK YOUR ANSWERS! ⟶

ANSWER KEY
CHECK YOUR ANSWERS!

Question #1

B. A group of jellyfish is called a "<u>smack.</u>"

 PLAYER 1 _____ /1

Question #2

A. The dirtiest thing in your house is your <u>TV remote.</u>

 PLAYER 1 _____ /1

Question #3

C. The <u>bobcat</u> is the most common wildcat in North America.

 PLAYER 2 _____ /1

Question #4

B. Elvis actually had <u>blonde hair</u>, but dyed it black.

 PLAYER 2 _____ /1

Round Total

TALLY UP YOUR POINTS! WHICHEVER PLAYER HAS THE LEAST AMOUNT OF POINTS HAS TO COMPLETE THE DARE BELOW.

PLAYER 1 _____ /2

PLAYER 2 _____ /2

DARE CHALLENGE

PUT JELLY BEANS BETWEEN YOUR TOES AND LEAVE THEM THERE FOR 10 MINUTES.

ROUND

5

 # PLAYER 1

CIRCLE THE FALSE STATEMENT IN EACH QUESTION.

Question #1

A. If sharks go upside down they will slip into a coma.

B. Girls are better at recognizing tastes than boys.

C. An owl has four different eyelids.

Question #2

A. Octopuses (Octopi) have 3 hearts and their blood is blue.

B. Jupiter is the hottest planet in our solar system.

C. On Venus, the planet, it actually snows metal!

PASS THE BOOK TO PLAYER 2 ⟶

PLAYER 2

CIRCLE THE FALSE STATEMENT IN EACH QUESTION.

Question #3

A. Beavers sleep while holding hands.

B. Spotted hyenas can digest skin and bones.

C. Geologist and educator, Florence Bascom, trained almost every female geologist of her time.

Question #4

A. The swan is known as the bird with the most feathers, with over 25,000 feathers.

B. Christopher Columbus believed the Earth was pineapple-shaped.

C. Cinderella is said to have been Walt Disney's favorite princess.

TIME TO CHECK YOUR ANSWERS! ⟶

ANSWER KEY
CHECK YOUR ANSWERS!

Question #1

C. An owl has <u>three</u> different eyelids; one for blinking, one for sleeping, and one for keeping the eyes clean and healthy.

 PLAYER 1 _____ /1

Question #2

B. <u>Venus</u> is the hottest planet in our solar system, reaching over 842° Fahrenheit!

 PLAYER 1 _____ /1

Question #3

A. <u>Otters</u> sleep while holding hands.

 PLAYER 2 _____ /1

Question #4

B. Christopher Columbus believed the Earth was <u>pear-shaped.</u>

 PLAYER 2 _____ /1

Round Total

TALLY UP YOUR POINTS! WHICHEVER PLAYER HAS THE LEAST AMOUNT OF POINTS HAS TO COMPLETE THE DARE BELOW.

 PLAYER 1 _____ /2

 PLAYER 2 _____ /2

DARE CHALLENGE

SMELL ONE OF THE OTHER PLAYER'S ARMPITS FOR AT LEAST 20 SECONDS.

ROUND

6

PLAYER 1

CIRCLE THE FALSE STATEMENT IN EACH QUESTION.

Question #1

A. Marilyn vos Savant has the highest IQ score in the entire world.

B. The first person to survive a trip over Niagara Falls in a barrel was Annie Edson Taylor.

C. Before 1900, shoes for the right and left foot were the same.

Question #2

A. Elephants can drink 30 gallons of water in one day!

B. Merida is the only princess not to have a solo or duet song in her movie.

C. Lionesses do 90% of the hunting for their prides, while lions mainly just protect.

PASS THE BOOK TO PLAYER 2 ⟶

PLAYER 2

CIRCLE THE FALSE STATEMENT IN EACH QUESTION.

Question #3

A. In the original Beauty and the Beast film, Belle was the only person to wear blue in her town.

B. The largest egg in the world belongs to the Beluga whale.

C. A flamingo can only eat when its head is upside down.

Question #4

A. Your toenails grow four times as fast as your fingernails.

B. Starfish actually have five eyes, one on the end of each leg.

C. Elsa's ice palace changes colors depending on her mood.

TIME TO CHECK YOUR ANSWERS! ⟶

ANSWER KEY
CHECK YOUR ANSWERS!

Question #1

C. Before <u>1800</u>, shoes for the right and left foot were the same.

 PLAYER 1   _____ /1

Question #2

A. Elephants can drink <u>50 gallons</u> of water in one day!

 PLAYER 1   _____ /1

Question #3

B. The largest egg in the world belongs to the <u>Whale shark.</u>

 PLAYER 2   _____ /1

Question #4

A. Your <u>fingernails</u> grow four times as fast as your toenails.

 PLAYER 2   _____ /1

Round Total

TALLY UP YOUR POINTS! WHICHEVER PLAYER HAS THE LEAST AMOUNT OF POINTS HAS TO COMPLETE THE DARE BELOW.

 PLAYER 1 _____ /2

 PLAYER 2 _____ /2

DARE CHALLENGE

DO THE FLOSS ON HIGH SPEED FOR 30 SECONDS.

ROUND

7

PLAYER 1

CIRCLE THE FALSE STATEMENT IN EACH QUESTION.

Question #1

A. Your mind is more active while you're awake than when you're dreaming.

B. There is a butterfly in Africa called the *Antimachus Swallowtail* and it has enough poison in its body to kill six cats!

C. A group of unicorns is also known as a "Blessing."

Question #2

A. Jasmine, from *Aladdin*, is the only princess not to be the main character in her film.

B. Girls, on average, fart more often than boys.

C. The first woman in America to receive a medical degree was Elizabeth Blackwell.

PASS THE BOOK TO PLAYER 2 ⟶

PLAYER 2

Question #3

A. Queen Elizabeth has two birthdays every year.

B. The first woman in space was Patricia Bath.

C. An elephant can smell water from up to 12 miles away.

Question #4

A. Katia Krafft, the pioneer of volcano nature photography, was killed by volcano lava changing direction.

B. Dogs have two different air passages, one is for breathing and the other for smelling.

C. Alice Ball was a biochemist and the first American woman to win a Nobel Prize in science.

TIME TO CHECK YOUR ANSWERS! ⟶

ANSWER KEY
CHECK YOUR ANSWERS!

Question #1

A. Your mind is <u>more active while you're dreaming</u> than when you're awake.

 PLAYER 1 _____ /1

Question #2

B. Both boys and girls fart, <u>no gender has proven to fart more often than the other.</u>

 PLAYER 1 _____ /1

Question #3

B. The first woman in space was <u>Valentina Tereshkova.</u>

 PLAYER 2 _____ /1

Question #4

C. <u>Gerty Cori</u> was a biochemist and the first American woman to win a Nobel Prize in science.

 PLAYER 2 _____ /1

Round Total

TALLY UP YOUR POINTS! WHICHEVER PLAYER HAS THE
LEAST AMOUNT OF POINTS HAS TO COMPLETE
THE DARE BELOW.

 PLAYER 1 _____ /2

 PLAYER 2 _____ /2

DARE CHALLENGE

STUFF A HANDFUL OF MARSHMALLOWS IN YOUR MOUTH AND SING 'TWINKLE TWINKLE LITTLE STAR'.

ROUND

8

PLAYER 1

CIRCLE THE FALSE STATEMENT IN EACH QUESTION.

Question #1

A. One of the first recorded women to study and teach math was Hypatia.

B. Cucumbers are actually a fruit and not a vegetable.

C. Emmy Noether was the first woman to be professionally employed as an electrical engineer in the U.S.

Question #2

A. Chien-Shiung Wu was deemed the "First Lady of Math."

B. Jane Cooke Wright was a pioneering cancer researcher who helped save millions of lives with her new chemotherapy techniques.

C. A "kid" is another name for a baby goat.

PASS THE BOOK TO PLAYER 2 ⟶

PLAYER 2

CIRCLE THE FALSE STATEMENT IN EACH QUESTION.

Question #3

A. Ariel was the first fictional character to get a star on the *Hollywood Walk of Fame*.

B. Womens brains are more interconnected and it is easier for them to use both sides of their brain, unlike men.

C. A hippopotamus produces milk that is bright pink.

Question #4

A. A unicorn's eyes can only be purple or sky-blue.

B. A group of whales is also known as a "puddle."

C. On average, girls are more talkative than boys.

TIME TO CHECK YOUR ANSWERS! ⟶

ANSWER KEY
CHECK YOUR ANSWERS!

Question #1

C. <u>Edith Clarke</u> was the first woman to be professionally employed as an electrical engineer in the U.S.

 PLAYER 1 _____ /1

Question #2

A. Chien-Shiung Wu was deemed the <u>**"First Lady of Physics."**</u>

 PLAYER 1 _____ /1

Question #3

A. <u>Snow White</u> was the first fictional character to get a star on the *Hollywood Walk of Fame.*

 PLAYER 2 _____ /1

Question #4

B. A group of whales is also known as a <u>"pod."</u>

 PLAYER 2 _____ /1

Round Total

TALLY UP YOUR POINTS! WHICHEVER PLAYER HAS THE LEAST AMOUNT OF POINTS HAS TO COMPLETE THE DARE BELOW.

 PLAYER 1 _____ /12

 PLAYER 2 _____ /12

DARE CHALLENGE

PICK SOMETHING IN THE ROOM AND WEAR IT ON YOUR HEAD FOR THE REST OF THE GAME!

PLAYER 1

CIRCLE THE FALSE STATEMENT IN EACH QUESTION.

Question #1

A. Women make up over 57% of the college degrees earned in the world.

B. Merida is only the second Disney princess to not have an American accent.

C. A unicorn horn is also called a "Maticorn."

Question #2

A. The most popular female dog name is Bella.

B. Rachel Carson, a conservationist, wrote her first book about birds when she was only 10-years-old.

C. It took more than three years to create and perfect Merida's curly hair.

PASS THE BOOK TO PLAYER 2 ⟶

PLAYER 2

CIRCLE THE FALSE STATEMENT IN EACH QUESTION.

Question #3

A. Jasmine and Mulan are the only princesses to wear pants.

B. Killer whales are actually a type of dolphin.

C. Cinderella loses her shoe not once, but twice in her movie.

Question #4

A. The most popular male dog name is Buddy.

B. Fish are actually able to cough.

C. "Armadillo" is actually a spanish word that means "little armored one."

TIME TO CHECK YOUR ANSWERS! ⟶

ANSWER KEY
CHECK YOUR ANSWERS!

Question #1

C. A unicorn horn is also called a <u>"Alicorn."</u>

 PLAYER 1 _____ /1

Question #2

B. Rachel Carson, a conservationist, wrote her first book about birds when she was only <u>8-years-old.</u>

 PLAYER 1 _____ /1

Question #3

C. Cinderella loses her shoe <u>3 times</u> in her movie.

 PLAYER 2 _____ /1

Question #4

A. The most popular male dog name is <u>Max.</u>

 PLAYER 2 _____ /1

Round Total

TALLY UP YOUR POINTS! WHICHEVER PLAYER HAS THE
LEAST AMOUNT OF POINTS HAS TO COMPLETE
THE DARE BELOW.

 PLAYER 1 _____ /2

 PLAYER 2 _____ /2

DARE CHALLENGE

ACT LIKE A CHICKEN AND GIVE
YOUR BEST "BAWK!" ANYTIME
SOMEONE SAYS YOUR NAME
DURING THE REST OF THE GAME.

ROUND

10

PLAYER 1

CIRCLE THE FALSE STATEMENT IN EACH QUESTION.

Question #1

A. Jellyfish do not have a brain, a heart or bones.

B. Both Pocahontas and Ariel were based off of an actual person.

C. Some ribbon worms will eat themselves if they cannot find food.

Question #2

A. Pigs can suffer from *Mysophobia*, also known as the fear of dirt.

B. Karen Horney discovered that a human's sex is determined by "X" and "Y" chromosomes.

C. The larvae of a ladybug look like tiny black alligators.

PASS THE BOOK TO PLAYER 2 ⟶

PLAYER 2

CIRCLE THE FALSE STATEMENT IN EACH QUESTION.

Question #3

A. Ohio was the first state to grant women the right to vote.

B. Some species of aquatic turtles can breathe through their butt!

C. Technically, Mulan is not actually a princess.

Question #4

A. Merida is the only princess to have brothers, instead of only sisters and stepsisters.

B. The word "peacock" is used to describe both the males and females.

C. The only planet to rotate on its side is Uranus.

TIME TO CHECK YOUR ANSWERS! ⟶

ANSWER KEY
CHECK YOUR ANSWERS!

Question #1

B. <u>Only Pocahontas</u> was based off of an actual person.

 PLAYER 1 _____ /1

Question #2

B. <u>Nettie Stevens</u> discovered that a human's sex is determined by "X" and "Y" chromosomes.

 PLAYER 1 _____ /1

Question #3

A. <u>Wyoming</u> was the first state to grant women the right to vote.

 PLAYER 2 _____ /1

Question #4

B. The word "peacock" is used to describe <u>only the males</u>. Females are called "peahens."

 PLAYER 2 _____ /1

Round Total

TALLY UP YOUR POINTS! WHICHEVER PLAYER HAS THE LEAST AMOUNT OF POINTS HAS TO COMPLETE THE DARE BELOW.

 PLAYER 1 _____ /2

 PLAYER 2 _____ /2

DARE CHALLENGE

SPIN AROUND 8-10 TIMES, THEN TRY TO WALK IN A STRAIGHT LINE.

Round Total

ADD UP ALL YOUR POINTS FROM EACH ROUND.
THE PLAYER WITH THE MOST POINTS IS CROWNED
THE ULTIMATE LIE DETECTOR!

IN THE EVENT OF A TIE, CONTINUE TO ROUND 11
FOR THE TIE-BREAKER ROUND!

PLAYER 1

_____
GRAND TOTAL

PLAYER 2

_____
GRAND TOTAL

_____

The Ultimate Lie Detector

ROUND

11

Tie-Breaker Round
(Winner Takes All!)

PLAYER 1

CIRCLE THE FALSE STATEMENT IN EACH QUESTION.

Question #1

A. Aurora, from *Sleeping Beauty,* is the quietest of all the princesses.

B. Marie Curie invented the word "Radioactivity."

C. Elsa is the tallest of all the Disney princesses.

Question #2

A. Unicorns are only female.

B. On average, humans lose 50-100 hairs a day.

C. A duck has more neck bones than a giraffe!

PASS THE BOOK TO PLAYER 2 ⟶

PLAYER 2

Question #3

A. Mature wolves in the wild don't bark, only the cubs will occasionally bark.

B. Women currently make up 44% of the active duty Army.

C. Erika Eiffel actually married the Eiffel Tower in 2008.

Question #4

A. According to a new study, mice actually do not like cheese.

B. Bats always turn left when they leave their cave.

C. Rapunzel's hair in *Tangled* is approximately 100-feet long.

TIME TO CHECK YOUR ANSWERS! ⟶

ANSWER KEY
CHECK YOUR ANSWERS!

Question #1

C. <u>Aurora</u> is the tallest of all the Disney princesses.

 PLAYER 1 _____ /1

Question #2

A. Unicorns can be <u>both male and female.</u>

 PLAYER 1 _____ /1

Question #3

B. Women currently make up <u>14%</u> of the active duty Army.

 PLAYER 2 _____ /1

Question #4

C. Rapunzel's hair in *Tangled* is approximately <u>70-feet long.</u>

 PLAYER 2 _____ /1

Round Total

TALLY UP YOUR POINTS! WHICHEVER PLAYER HAS THE MOST POINTS IS CROWNED

THE ULTIMATE LIE DETECTOR!

THE PLAYER WITH THE LEAST AMOUNT OF POINTS HAS TO COMPLETE THE FINAL DARE. IF SCORES RESULT IN A TIE, BOTH PLAYERS MUST COMPLETE THE DARE!

PLAYER 1 _____ 12

PLAYER 2 _____ 12

The Ultimate Lie Detector

DARE CHALLENGE

SING YOUR FAVORITE SONG IN THE HIGHEST VOICE POSSIBLE.

CHECK OUT OUR

Visit us at
www.DontLaughChallenge.com
to check out our newest books!

OTHER JOKE BOOKS!

If you have enjoyed our book, we would love for you to review us on Amazon!

Made in the USA
Middletown, DE
11 December 2020